A Swatch of Twilight

MODERN LIBRARY OF INDONESIA

ACEP ZAMZAM NOOR

A Swatch of Twilight

Selected Poems

translated by
John H McGlynn

Jakarta, Indonesia

Contents

Pangrango, 1

Wind and Rock, 2

Chant, 3

My Melancholy Blues, 6

With the Grass, I Weep, 7

Solitude, 8

Melancholia, 9

The Poet's Earth, 10

Evening Song, 11

Cipasung, 12

Pastoral, 13

Lovers, 14

Trasimeno, 15

Arco Etrusco, 17

Rive and Estuary, 19

Above Umbria, 20

Paesaggio, 22

The Rain Has Died, 24

Kumbasari Market, Denpasar, 26

For Lina Sagaral Reyes, 28

Never to Die, 30

A Swatch of Twilight, 31

Trail, 34

A Poet Once More, 36

The Mountain's Breath, 38

A Story for Imana Tahira, 39

For Malika Hamoudi, 41

Yet to Come, 43

Age, 45

Soccer, 46

Secrets, 47

On Malioboro, 48

Love's Force, 49

Like Death Approaching, 50

Like Love and Death, 51

Pilgrimage to Londa, 52

Night in Toraja, 54

On Southern Waves, 56

I Want To Be With You, 59

My Poems, 60

Lessons from the Gulf, 62

A Part of Joy, 63

The Prayers of a Flower Farmer, 66

Northern Ode, 67

Climbing the Hill of Prayer, 68

Coconut Tart, 69

An Episode Repeated, 70

After the Drizzle, 71

Galunggung's Message, 72

I Thought, 73

Talisé Shore, 74

In the Direction of Donggala, 75

Sulamadaha, 76

Tapulaga, 77

There Are No More Twilights, 78

Impressions of Liu Sanjie, 80

Reading the Signs, 82

Crossing to Bokori, 83

Sagaraanakan, 84

Nusakambangan, 85

Amazing, 86

I Welcome the Sun, 87

Nipah Bay, 88

About A Poet, 89

One Step from your Heart, 90

The Language of Longing, 91

Monument to Resolution, 92

Come Low Tide, 93

Twilight's Tongue, 94

Self-talk 1, 95

Self-talk 2, 96

Self-talk 3, 97

Self-talk 4, 98

Self-talk 5, 99

Self-talk 6, 100

About Schedules, 101

One Morning at Karet Bivac Cemetery, 103

From the Window of Le Meridien, 104

Past Cibatu Station, 105

Glossary of Names and Geographical Locations, 113

An Interview with the Poet, 117

Biographical Information, 131

Pangrango

Here it is
When firs shed their needles
Trees are surprised. We see it
As the fleet wind
Hastens in our direction

We hear it
When downcast clouds descend
In Pangrango it only rains
While the wind in the haze over the mount
Continues its approach towards twilight

When traversing the forest of memory
When feeing alone. We count it
From here where longing flows
Past paddy fields and boulders
Between home and this quixotic adventure

Wind and Rock

1

Why must rocks be silent
And not the wind? A rock is solid and cold
Yet can seethe like fire
In its gut flows a river and the solemnity
Of prayer. He is silent and mute
But at once thunderous

2

Why not the wind
Why must the rock? He is tempered by time
Made ripe by longing

Chant

I float
Lightly
Ascending to you. I am cotton dancing
In the wind
A fish somersaulting
A tongue of fire

My breath is foul, Anne
From the hundreds of years of calling
Your name

This is my chant:
Molten asphalt of my neglect, liquefied lead
Of my faults, thundering machine of my wildness
Trash heap of my downfall
Clogged gutter of my futility

I am drowsy but cannot sleep, hungry
But cannot eat, thirsty
But cannot drink, sad
But cannot cry, wounded
But cannot treat myself, bereft
But cannot take my life

Anne! Anne! Anne!

My chant is a thousand silences impaling you
Breaking through the sheath of your sky, demolishing
Your cloud clusters, scorching the turbulence
Of your fog, immolating the distance
Between space and time

I liquify
Like water
And flow to you. Like rain
Spilt to earth
Tumbling like a stone
Or a ghost

Anne! Anne! Anne!

This is the crackling gunfire of my longing, the launch
Of my grenade of feat, the echoing gunshot of my drunkenness
The overflowing oil of my passion, the smoldering hearth
    of my love
The smoking clouds of my extinction

I am poor but do not beg, in pressing need
But do not steal, in grevious debt but do not plunder
Even with ample opportunity, do not engage in deceit
Though well within my rights, make no demands
Despite having no other recourse, use no force

Anne! Anne! Anne!

My chant is a thousand silences chasing after you
Knocking down the barricade of your defenses, breaking through
The walls of your confinement, turning upside down the place
Of your meditation, destroying the throne
Of your solemnity

My breath smells foul, Anne
From the hundreds of years
Of calling your name

My Melancholy Blues

1

I am still sailing, following the wind's draft
Cutting through twilight's secrets. Not to the estuary
Does my journey lead, nor to your heart
I have traversed all rivers and every sea
Swallowed drunkenly. Birthed a thousand poems
Creating pools of tears:
With steps growing more distant and unsteady

2

I shall reaffirm our distance:
Forget the purity of love created from a thousand prayers
Having the same downfall in that same shallowness.
Wash your face with what's left of my tears
Or conceal it within my dark poems
The world is in movement, shedding its dark cloak
Twilight thickens, night hardens like stone

3

Alright then, I will kneel in prayer before dawn arrives
But without remorse for unavoidable mistakes
My voice still nestling within the pounding of the waves
As long as the the sky hosts the sun
In the name of ancient truths and lies
Immolate my poems and forget me:
Morning's light appearing with the truth of time

With the Grass, I Weep

With the grass, I weep
My birth was marked by dewdrops
And a mist that cleansed me
Behind the mountain, the wind taught me
To speak in the name of silence

With ducks, I count the days
With stones, I understand cold and silence
My steps are the tracks of a snail
My voice yearns for the horizon
Screaming for a blue sky

I drink the sap of time
Dark clouds pile over me so that I may dream
The air teaches me to read
I understand the book of seasons and weather
My language, that of the river flowing to its mouth

With moss, I meditate
With rippling water, I dance
My prayer, the setting sun
My solemnity, the rising moon
Reaching for its peak

Solitude

Near waves constantly speaking your name
I forget the moon's trail that once lighted my way
A thousand spears dart from fishermen's torches
Fireflies vie to set me alight at night's edge
Without faith in what I hear, I keep my eyes shut

The quietest thing might be that rebounding light
Very like the sound of caves
Shimmering like a knife rubbed against the heart
When again I try to speak your name,
I slowly drown in the gentle stabs of dawn

The stones meditating on the banks of your veins
Seem to have discovered a new land in my solitude
Dawn puts an end to the reading of dark verses
With morning's arrival, the stars have dimmed
I call out for no one, accepting my solitude

Melancholia

An alley divides night's dense darkness:
There you will walk alone
To meet your destiny. A dying lantern
With weary light hardly flickers bright enough
To reveal the nodding shadows of wild bushes
Growing around the grave. Go there
Where, trembling, you will caress your fate
Embracing an eternal solitude

A footpath cuts through the wilderness
Where you passed your days and later froze:
It is there I will walk alone
Silent and unsmiling. The wooden cane
Found to be of no further use
You threw into the rapids. You must walk alone
Without cane or lantern
Continuing to walk despite all doubt

The Poets' Earth

For us the earth was unfurled
Trees planted to support the sky's roof
The poets' blue sky
Rivers feed into us, into patience
There is no dry season for honest emotion
The sun warms only morning's affection
Affectionately, we cuddle with the earth
The poet's earth is a wide-open one
Where paddy fields produce poetry
And rice stalks sway with song

For us, this expanse was unfurled
Both a motherland and a home
We sow our seed and irrigate our words
Orchards grow in our hearts and good intentions
From the sky, rain pours
Grass grows on our beds
A soft mattress and a thick blanket
A mattress for our union with the universe
The passion released manifests as beauty
The children born transform into poems

Evening Song

Rays of sunlight slipping between a mosque's dome
And the silhouette of a stand of bamboo
Mountains sleeping in the faded blue distance
A stream with clear waters rushes through boulders' clefts
Muted as a muezzin's call wrapped in thin mist
My home, all that I long for, buried beneath mute years
Now I want to create a poem for you

A yellow carpet stretching into the distance
Paddy fields and broken lines of green dikes
In the north the protracted calamity is long past
The destruction now to be found in memory
The change of seasons presents another green
Crimson flowers brighten leaves wet with dew
The oxcart still dragging its burden to the south

On this so very quiet verandah, it is the heart that speaks
Amid steam from hot coffee and clouds of cigarette smoke
Increasingly ensnared not by grief or hunger
Or by tortured allegiances
We are ever more feeling the loss of a home called time
The sky darkens, rivers return to their estuaries
Leaves move slowly with the wind, and the fog thickens

As talk about flower bushes in the yard continues
Galunggung stands mighty in the faded blue distance
The call of the muezzin trembling with the drizzle
While neighbors' gardens still talk of simplicity
The smiles of girls and women coming home from ablutions
My wife and I ever more isolated, not from loss of space
We ask too much of life

Cipasung

In the curve of your eyebrows, rice fields yellow
Like my hair, paddy sheathes bow ever lower
With the rice I also harvest your heart's patience
My hoe is faith and my prayer mat the thick mud
The sky testing my devotion drips faded light
My prayer hut burnt by a silence inflamed with longing

Though ever closer I come to the extinction this world promises
I still plant the days' seeds in fields of bitterness
All plants and trees bear forth fresh rewards
The bamboo fences my faith has erected
Come close to me, hearing the chants of fish
My heart now a pool storing your purity

Tomorrow my journey as a farmer begins
Opening charity's fields in the deep wilderness
Attempting to understand the ever more real path of nonexistence
Long have I weighed the world and repeatedly destroyed it
Without rice seedlings and still wishing to harvest that other
patience of yours
On the prayer mat of mud, I collapse and am buried

Pastoral

The fog entrapping you
Has dissipated into words
All that's left of the wooden house
Is its chill and the silence now fallen there

Death is not the slowly descending fog
But snow flakes
That flit about like time
And stop your breathing

Depart and don't look back
I want to witness your naked body
With no overcoat of conviction
Growing distant, ever more distant

The mosque's dome and the cathedral's spire
Drown behind the mountain
Twilight thickens in my glass of coffee
Which I gulp like a bitter poem

Depart and do not cry
Night's torch will be your escort
As you traverse the path of patience
And make your way through the forest

Death is not words
But a prayer
Shinining like the light of heaven
And suddenly burning

Lovers

Attar sang of birds taking wing
From branches of the soul
Sana'i planted and plucked everlasting roses
Many were the songs and songs as well
Whispered by the wind when praising Solomon's compassion
Stones polished by lovers become true sapphires
The air filling with the scent of hearts on fire

When hearing David's sweet ballads
Trees instantly ceased falling to the ground
The sky's tears crystallized midair
Rumi invited the sun to descend from his heart
Grasses surprised by their bond to roots
The earth's soul moved in a light dance
Stones flying about like cotton

Around the Mediterranean's fresh waters
The sky was like metal burnished with gold
It was there that Jonah sculpted his poems in calligraphy
Ones difficult to decipher, yet both fish and lizards
could read them, even with their eyes closed
Coral outcroppings shrank into grains of sand
The sea opening the pages of a book

Hafiz fermented grapes from the orchard of his heart
Then invited birds to become drunk together
Jami swayed his hips between two large goblets
The sky and earth offering to life
There is no telling how many songs and tears
Washing down secret rivers to Safa and Marwa
Becoming a wave of lovers

Trasimeno

A lake
A large blue prayer rug
Is a calm unequaled:
Wind and fog, a row of pines
Hills loosening their locks
Beneath a vermillion sky

The lake's surface
Is not disturbed by the sound of insects
Gray clouds rise like a veil from a hearth
Wrappping themselves around twilight
Before me, the water becomes a prayer rug
Somewhere between blue and deep green

A balcony, table, and a chair
Form a silent conversation:
Poetry and perplexity are ever present
In my solitude. Poetry pools like water
Poetry floats in the frozen air
Poetry leads me close to you

A face without form
Mysterious shadows transforming
In the gloaming. I perform my prayers
In harbors and in boats
In the far distant past
In all manner of places and in solitude

I see the hills in genuflection
Trees, electric poles
Wind and fog thickening and rolling
All in genuflection before you. A lake
A prayer rug for the universe
A perfect calm

Arco Etrusco

Our solitude
Built from a pile of stones
And dark tunnels
Metal arches and cathedral
Spires. Our solitude grows
Moss like a wall
Terraces of time
Rising ever higher

A limestone cliff is not as sheer
Emotions soar into space.
We count the steps
Discovering the signs
Of a long and wretched journey
Stars do not grow in a copper sky
While gardens have disappeared
Into earth. All that is left is children
Jumping into gaping chasms
On the wall of wind can be read
The silence of clouds, of rain trapped
In the air. We then witness everything
Buildings constructed and demolished
Roads winding like words
Trees stiffening and shrinking
Though the sun still burns the earthly hollows
Corpses arise from the dead
All that is our solitude

Constructed from the rubble of homes
The muteness of doors
Neighborhood alleyways and labyrinths
Of no end. Our solitude
Blackens statues
Becoming dark sentences
Forever read through eyes crackled
By time.

River and Estuary

Loneliness has convinced us
Every corner of the world has a dark side
Different from others. In the trembling of your hand
I can feel a season's chill unable to entirely extinguish the sun
In my eyes you see a rapidly slowing rain
We embrace, two seasons meeting
In the same loneliness. We light the fireplace in our room
Torching all our clothing and beliefs
Turning them to smoke filling space and time

We do not invite the snow to fall, dampening our bed
But seconds pool from our drops of sweat
Exploring each curve in your body is like feeling
Every nook of this earth. I slip on earth's sloping hemispheres
Lose my breath in another section of rolling hills
You touch my drought with your springtime hand
Until grasses grow green over my entire body
We kiss like the meeting of river and estuary
Filling and releasing each other, all at once.

Above Umbria

In the afternoon
Strands of light
Blown by the summer wind
Seem to paint the sky's face
With silver lines
A bell swings in the air
Its sound next to silent. A horse vaults
Stands of grass to a death unseen
Light lies low on the mountains
The sun puts its wick over stones
Fruit ripening in the light. I touch
Your windblown hair and see an abyss
In the depths of your eyes:
A naked woman beneath the sun
Legs extended into the lake

I recall distant tropical shores
With yellowish-green women
Like mangoes. I imagine fresh young coconut milk
Then lying on my back beneath the sun
Naked beneath your thorny gaze:
Here, the trees bear the words' fruits
Each one a kindness as well as a grievous sin
I don't know how you plant your words in the soil
Turning them into advice. While your ivory body
Responds with cement pillars, spans of electric wire,
Black and gleaming asphalt roads in the distance
I see a train on its track crawling steadfastly through time
Tunnels appearing in every direction

A white horse
A mysterious voice hovering in the air
Is the broken statue of a god. I plant my hand
My neck lengthens as I sow my thoughts on the field
I wring out my blood, fermenting its pure poison
Drunkenness is a path climbing the earth:
Creeping between towering bottles
I sing my sacred mantras to the cosmos
Fruits glow with my touch
Land becoming fertile and lustful
And then as with other allegorical beings
You suddenly burn me with truth
Fireworks exploding from your flaming breast

Paesaggio

One day on a peninsula:
My lithe memory climbed the limestone cliff
Thrusting itself outward, dangling
From the beard of a tree and an eagle's wing
Diving and breaking itself apart midair
A shower of sulfur

The past constructs a bridge
From grains of sand and water
A typhoon sweeps away tents in the south
Roots and grasses dry on the plain
Standing against the sky and the blue sea
A miraculous kiss ends our conversation

My years are scattered among many cities
Accompanied by weary sweat, blood, and cum
Summertime sways with its solar axe
The sea covered with the silver light of day
I hear the clash of waves and light
Silence growing shrill, winged

Across the island, where every fall is eternal
Women dance with fiery hair
Men spin amid clouds of smoke
All drunk and writhing
We once built a fire tower from words
Before everything fell, returning to silence

From the charred remains and those glimmering days
I gathered shards of glass, ceramic, metal, and poems
Arrogance, plus feelings of uselessness
The dry season swings its axe all day long
The sun appearing all powerful and thorny:
My memory aroused, moved, exploded

The Rain has Died

The rain has died,
Again, the rain has died
Throughout the rainy season
When the air is completely frozen
My blood freshens, like a clock
Floating on the wooden floor:
I can't say which is more beautiful
The reality of time past or the broken lines
Of my memory. But I must find another place
For the light of these words to fade
Tomorrow, when the sun appears from behind the hill
My hand will reach for the nearest strand of your hair

The rain has died
Here, again, the rain has died
The fireplace in the living room
The sound of burning coal
Is the final sign of silence:
A pair of shoes is not the only world
A pile of letters, telephone cards, and electric bills
Only a part of your small room in the city
Now my words struggle to resist slogans and rhetoric
Amid the blare of the television and the cold of the refrigerator
In time, when newspapers announce your death
One of my kisses will redden the horizon's full cheek

The rain has died
Again, my love, the rain has died
So calmly beside the bread
Maybe I am still in the kitchen, cooking
The moment my thoughts explore jungles and museums:
The train has taken me to the most secret corners
Of all the civil wars raging there
But just a hand's length from your navel I discovered that beauty
    mark
And then life, too, I could conclude quickly
Now, when bombs are falling and exploding
In our bed we can still embrace, perspiring lightly

Kumbasari Market, Denpasar

Likely it's not the moonlight
Illuminating the river's surface
All across the bridge near the market
Sellers of fish, meat, and vegetables
Seem to make night eternal. The market is thunder
At once a meditation of voices
I see the sellers begin to dance
The coolies begin to sing
One and all of them, women—
The chill permeating their sweat
Turns it into bottles of arrack

Here, the women are men
For whom work is prayer and dance
With them, I shoulder the baskets
While distilling my own sweat
Into the power of words
I drink arrack mixed with cold dew
Asking the moonlight
To cast its yellow sash on me
Among them, I dance wildly
Praising the trees' tendrils and stone markers
Love-drunk and waiting for dawn to arrive

One ceremony after another, I go through
Forgetting myself the length of my journey
Along with vegetables and flower offerings
Pork, fish, incense, and colorful cloth
I become part of both the market's thunder

The silence of meditation . . .
Slowly, words dripping from my sweat
Words changing to grains of salt
Becoming spice for land and river
Where those mighty women
Finish their dances and obligations
As normal human beings

For Lina Sagaral Reyes

Your fate is a bullet
Fired into the air:
A fountain, the source of pure words
Among black stones, tree roots, and cracked earth
The sun is created from the purity of words
The sky's tears crystallize tops of palms
The energy of words. A thick dam cracked
A volcano about to explode
The river has sent your voice
To distant and silent estuaries
Your words will harden
Like waves
Salted by time

In the valleys of your virgin land
The sky takes off its robe
I inhale the aroma of humus and the scent of mud
Imagining golden grass flowers
Who could be the owner of a land
As large as this? I have found no one here
Just a flooded lake:
A small island, white swans, a boat
Green waters with polite ripples
No croaking of frogs, no clinking piano
There is only you, Lina, with a bullet in your chest
Breathing in water, algae, and the chill of stones

Who is it that controls this nameless expanse
Of land and water? I hear no sound of speeches
I see no lengthy processions
Of soldiers coming and going like the night
A major war or a minor conflict, rubble, corpses
A catastrophic earthquake will finish everything:
In the wilderness of your country that is now on fire
Wild horses no longer race
Feral dogs are asleep
Trees bow their heads
A yellow man on a limestone hill
His voice is shrill like your silence
Slammed by a thousand bullets

Never to Die

I have entered every closure
Offering silence
All chasms inviting me
To kill myself. I have drunk all poisons
Darkness has offered
Chewed on the wind and foul weather
Screaming silently
Together with bats I've grown drunken
Collapsing behind a wave

I followed the storm's bidding
Throwing me into space
I've slept in all the beds of clouds
Sown my seed with the rain
In my emptiness, I swallowed the years
Released from the almanac of time
The seasons have broken all my bones
My sweat spatters the fields
My blood floats in the frozen air

The moon is not my destination
Nor are the stars scattered here
I must go forward in order to collapse again
Dive into the nameless sea
Everything the typhoon has to offer
I must welcome willingly
There is something more delightful than death
It matters not if I suffer alone forever
Chased from one silence to another

Screaming, never to die

A Swatch of Twilight

I give to you a swatch of rose-colored twilight
A bundle of clouds and a handful of intoxicating fog
I am yet unable to translate into poetry
Your smile is too mischievous for a woman of fine faith
Your shoulders not stooped enough
For you to be limping through Basra's lanes with a staff
For me, solitude is insufficient to give birth to a poem
We have truly not been burned in fire

Often you have called me a crazed Hamlet
Only for my doubt in interpreting the look in your eyes
All the time I needed to continue running
Before smearing my canvases with tears
Perhaps I more closely resemble the accursed Sisyphus
Or the drunken Narcissus? I give to you a swatch of twilight
A bundle of clouds and a handful of intoxicating fog
Which I am yet unable to express in painting

In the tunnels of Mecca
I write nothing, paint no one either
In the arrid dunes, in the stony hills
I neither wail nor sing; I only read silence
I am not Bilal loudly voicing the call to prayer
Nor am I that daredevil Hamzah, at the frontmost line
I am no one. My poetic creativity is only in my heart
I continue to run with that swatch of twilight I have to give

In the canals of Venice, beneath the arches of frail bridges
Among the tourists and pilgrims, and priests and prostitutes as well
 I never forget to call your name, and never forget
To curse you as well. Opening an ancient map on a restaurant table
Imagining a troop of horses galloping from the the south
Unrolling my canvases on the sidewalk, plastering papers
On a row of poles. Never, it turns out, have I forgotten
Your curly hair peeking from your yellow-green veil

You once ridiculed me as a pious coward
When I was shocked to hear that you wanted to go to Aceh
To follow in the footsteps of Tjut Njak Dien with a small lantern
Were you seeking the most point, the most distant edge
The most silent place? But your eyebrows are too beautiful for the
    jungle
For hunting meaning in the middle of the wilderness
Even though you might be welcomed in Lhok Nga with
tambourines
And showered with bouquets of flowers

Suddenly I collapse in the valley of Mina
My naked body wrapped in nothing but a white cloth
Like the sun, the air, the tents, all
White. Will the lambs hear my painful shrieks
Giving their blood to congeal my wounds? Will
Camels catch the acrid scent of my paint? Will the stony hills
Read my longing, bowling a boulder
With which to crush me? Will the sand dunes understand my
curses?

I give to you a swatch of rose-colored twlight
A bundle of clouds and a handful of intoxicating fog
I am yet unable to translate into poetry
Your breasts are too soft for a Marilyn Monroe
Your lips not thick enough for you to be forever smiling
While waving your hand about with a cigar between your fingers
For me, beauty is insufficient to bring forth a poem
We have not been truly drowned in silence

Trail

One terrace after another I climb
As if tracking the sharp days of old age
Suddenly, a friend from the past appears
He has wavy hair and the wings of an angel
A beautiful body but on his head a crown of thorns
He walks slowly, his voice resembling that of a shepherd
We meet on top of a hill, looking down below:
The month of July reflects off the winding road
In the distance bluish clumps of pine trees
Rooftops of homes and a church appear to hang in mid-air

My friend says little but his eyes glow
The afternoon light igniting sparks of flame from his hair
His breath makes the year tremble, causing olive leaves to wilt
From the center of his eyes vultures emerge, passing
Like migrants. My friend is not a prophet
His chest a thick wall called ideology
His strong legs supporting centuries of silence
In the past, my friend was the most sentimental of souls
With a smile capable of melting anyone's heart
Now he is leading me into a dark tunnel

Many altars have I had to leave behind
My sentences so often changing into others' voices
In that room for devotion full of moans and cries
I greet the congregation, forever feeling nauseous
Knowing that love must end so quickly:

A speech erupts among the roar of tanks and cannon fire
Canals overflow with flood and people moving to the right
I see my friend among them, hoisting corpses
Leaving behind for his followers a long trail
I quickly turn to the left, hastily leave

A Poet Once More

At Karang Setra Hotel, Melva, I found hairs of yours
On its slick ceramic floor. Whenever I see advertisements
For soap, shampoo, and toothpaste and anytime I see
Dangdut singers on television, Melva, I always think of you
Now alone in this hotel I feel myself to be
A poet once more, the intoxicating scent of your perfume
Suddenly slipping through the bathroom door
Attacking me like lines of poetry
You know, Melva, words always make me tremble
As do strange odors from your nape, neck, and armpits
Transforming into imagery

Now alone in this hotel I feel myself to be
A poet once more, carefully placing
Your brownish-colored hairs on the table with
My papers, cigarettes, a glass of coffee. I write a poem
Feeling your lips full in my mouth
Your voice continuing to fill my ears and mind
I write a poem thinking of the color of your shoes
Your underwear, your bra, and the belt
You once left behind, beneath my bed
A way of saying good bye

No, Melva, a poet does not feel sad for having been left
And feels no pain from forever losing
A poet doesn't cry for being betrayed
And does not faint when his mouth is silenced

A poet dies when he loses the power of words
Their potency morphing into prose:
Say, for instance, a never ending war
Piracy, plane crashes, floods, and earthquakes
Or this country's never ending corruption
The unrest, the looting, rape, and other such stuff

Oh, I am here, alone, feeling myself to be a poet once more

The Mountain's Breath

Like twilight kneeling at the foot of the sky
I praise your eyes that melt the fading light
And the indistinct letters that spell out
Eternity. Your smile hanging in the air
Is sheltered by a clump of reddish clouds
With trembling lips I cannot catch
The drops of dew rolling from your tongue.

Your veil releases the mountain's breath
Turning rice fields to green in my heart
The prayer mat unrolled by longing
Makes me collapse again. I inhale the earth's fragrance
I smell the roots of the grass and cold stones:
A man bathed in blood
Being stabbed by your eyelashes

Pull back the tip of your veil, Dini
So that the sky can reveal the secret of its beauty
To the world. Your face, illuminated by moonlight
Your fine hair, brushed smooth by the wind
Seems to reveal all that has been concealed
That is the reason I praise your eyes
Like a thousand moths swarming around
A single lamp

A Story for Imana Tahira

Gazing at the sky
I think of the deep red
Face of power. When treading this earth
I seem to hear my silent voice

On the footpath
This honest earth provides
My words grow from air
Building high towers
Which, inevitably, collapse

My words
Cannot demolish the sky
 (nor can my cough or aching back)
They become water
Twisting to become a part
Of earth's sadness

On this footpath
Hemmed by the expanse of twilight sky
I hear a grain of sand
Speak to the powers:
"Take it, take all of it!"

A poet is a grain of sand
Who counts the seconds
Compressing words of discovery
Absorbing the earth's power

Then goes back to building towers
From water and air
Which, inevitably, collapse

My words
Can not demolish a power
As great and expansive
As the sky

But like a river
My words continue to flow
Through the earth's wilderness
In search of green estuaries
Following the trees' veins,
Absorbed by soil and stones

On this footpath
Hemmed in by a deep red sky
The poet again speaks to the powers:
"Take it, take all of it!"

For Malika Hamoudi

I watch your supple fingers and see in the sky
A procession of clouds sending another twilight
In our direction. Colors of red and pale blue
Clumps of gray floating in the far distance
From the window, I see the Seine dividing the city
Its many bridges filled with filigree carvings
Resembling your curly hair. Then, from the top of an apartment
    building
We jump—twisting, turning, screaming in the air:
Twilight shatters into thousands of silent signals
Translating either as desire
Or a suppressed wish for suicide

I still remember your belly dance, imagining
Your slim figure and chiseled features, the Algerian eyebrows
That stabbed this poet. In the train car,
In the tunnels boring through the body of this old city
There were those floundering from a loss of words
When silence proffered a rose-colored verandah
Termed muteness. So what was the meaning of our conversation
Between one stop and the next, as we traversed the winding streets
Went in and out of restaurants, museums, and book stores
When what I found was never space? So it is
I understand destiny's wild movements, the first and final judgment
The betrayal later becoming a famous monument
Like the Bastille constantly busy with visitors

Beneath the light of mercury lamps, between marble poles
We feel ourselves to be even older than the earth's real age
With your chiseled features and sharp and gleaming stare
It looked as if you wanted to kill me. But death had already gone East
To the mountain slopes, to gloomy Montmartre
Now as my hand slowly touches your chin, I suddenly feel
Another kind of sharpness:
Why does such incredible beauty always unsheathe
A dagger? Like twilight implanting a response
I could never possibly express to you
Never possibly write on your underwear

Yet to Come

I watch as the sun drowns itself
As a chill sows the scent of wheat, and a whirlwind
Of old memories continuously twirls
In the heart of air. Snow has yet to come
The sky is blanketed with darkened clouds
Floating boats
Restaurants with dimmed lights
Closed museums. There are no angels
No sellers of cotton candy
Just a lone woman
With colorful apparel
And anklets with bells. A miserable December
A sad end of the year
Shambling towards a bar

Breathing in the air
Exploring the cobblestone lanes
I go forward with two minds:
As if again catching the scent of ink, piles of papers
Copper blocks, an old printing machine
In an atelier. But smelling as well the public toilet
The train station, the line of push bikes
And a pub with wooden walls
On the city's outskirts

Snow has yet to come
Leaves grow yellow on roof tops
Houses one on top of another
Like loudspeakers. A church is now a house

People pray wherever
Worship wherever, make love
Wherever

I circle about
And continue to circle
Following the chiming bells
Dissolving what's left of my conviction
Of something non-existent. Snow has yet to come
The angels have yet to pass,
Death like the shard of a green planet
Fluttering about. There is no conversation
No news from the islands
Just the tips of my shoes
Dragging themselves along the sidewalk
Having already spoken in the name of time,
About time

Age

An island
Turning white in night's mane
The miracle of a soundless season
Carved in the stillness
Of a copper sky

The glory of rain
With shafts of light
Stored far out at sea
A crestless surge
An echo with no reply
Dissolving
In the depths
Of time

Centuries of wind
Years of fog
Pure nights
Between birth
And the fall
We are naked souls
Living on a coral atoll

Soccer

At the age of 45, the man wrote some words
On a piece of paper, which then hung perplexedly
From a floral arrangement: "I long for you
As I once longed for Inne Ratu
When the entire sky was still blue"

Almost dusk, becak bells clanging at the crossroads
Dim lights flickering near the guard post, as an old banyan
Topples in the grounds of the kindergarten. The man stares
At the entrance to the lane, the row of homes, and the madrasah
As far as the turn in the road where someone is concealed

At the age of 45, words which he had once arranged
Continue to echo in his chest cavity, striking his ribs
Between coughs and asthma. "I love you
As I once loved Inne Ratu
When I felt there was no problem with time"

Time is a sports arena, it seems:
So many fields, so many players, but all ending
In defeat or victory. The man then walked, alone
Down the darkend road, towards the stadium
Playing a game of soccer with silence

Secrets

From the strands of your hair, birds fall
Into a painting; in the calm features
Of your perfect face, wet brushstrokes curve gently
Around full cheeks, your tapered chin. Brushstrokes, faintly flowing
Into the hollow of your ear, descending your long neck
That brilliant marble column. Beads of perspiration
Hang like a necklace between two sweet mounds
Where, deep inside your chest, secrets remain secrets

Fireflies alight on your shoulder, disappearing
Into a poem. Beneath, blood's flow seems to have ceased
How incredible is the beauty of a stifled gasp,
Of eyes slowly squeezed tightly shut. How great the devotion
Gleaned from repeated prayer and meditation
The point where the body opens all its secret doors
To the explorer of silence. Where years feel short,
Like minutes released with each emission of breath

On Malioboro

Amid the train cars heading east
And the scream of the train whistle still ringing in the ear
The air seems to tremble, though the rain has long stopped
We go outside, leaving that row of benches behind
Immediately visible are a slickened street, a bare sidewalk,
A stretch of track whose distant end is swallowed by darkness
You're a little tipsy from imbibing the opium of my words
While my face has turned blue with half-formed sentences
From short stories you have yet to finish writing

At a food stall everything begins to unfold
Like an old magazine. I remember again your name
Write down your address, count your moles, and interpret
Your signals. The image of a green butterfly above your breast
Leads me to believe that you are a descendent of fairies,
Your face a picture of beauty. Maybe your eyebrows aren't as even
As the bridge across the space separating your curved brows
But your hair, which is as messy as the rainy season and as foliate as a phras
Makes my breathing uncertain

When you kiss me like a soft and slow earthquake
I return your kiss like arid soil
Suddenly blessed by rain. Your lips taste of copper
Pungent like blood in the froth of your saliva
Which I swallow readily, as if wanting to consume
All that life holds. But in that open-air food stall
In the old magazine whose pages have begun to tatter
Your story is too brief for a lengthy love tale
In a city forever submerged in sadness

Love's Force

When your name penetrates my pores
I feel my blood stop flowing
The air trembles, not because of the distance of the morning
    horizon
But because of the sky's display of twilight's beauty
In the cleft of your breasts. When your voice courses through my
    veins
I hear islands to the southeast make ready to leave
And then, when your breath makes my heart palpitate
Ships sink out at sea, waves rise to throw themselves
On the land, a windstorm slams into the mountain.
The world is in chaos, not from the fire of jealousy
But from love showing its force

Like Death Approaching

For some reason, twilight seems simple
When seen through the windowpane.
Like a river separating forest from town
Like trawlers cutting through thick fog
Like logs on the river, moving slowly
For some reason, twilight seems simple
When seen through the windowpane
Like death approaching without a word

Like Love and Death

1

Beauty in the form of thick and brownish black eyebrows
A pierced nose and cracked lips resembling copper
A sweet sound is heard in the isolated moans, in sighs of silence,
In the resoluteness standing watch over bed and sofa
Dangerous moments suddenly appear when vowels make present
The sound of an utterance. Stillness swiftly descends when sentences
Drown letters, turning them into consonants,
Only read and understood by the silence of morning

2

Elegance sculpts the limestone mount into a nude statue
With large breasts like those of an ancient monument
Balance carves the curve of the wave on its broad back
And around its waist. Stand in the gloaming silently
And see how death's approach resembles the movement of a ballerina
An elderly dancer who gaily disseminates into the world
Both allure and disaster. Beauty and death exchange calls
Reverberating in the echoes of one ocean and another

3

Devotion is like a mountain climber scaling a curly head of hair
Traversing everlasting aerial roots. Death is like a mischievous surfer
Speeding through lanes of blood, following the breaks in breathing
Crossing the heart's verandah. Resignation is pictured in hospital rooms,
Maternity wards. Birth and death are like twins with different miens
Kept distant from each other for so long, but who will meet again
In time. Like lovers who are fated to remain far apart
Like love and death which do in fact yearn for each other

Pilgrimage to Londa

Climbing the winding stairway
I arrive at the top of the steep cliff
Engrave the line of a poem
In an ebony tree. Something vague
Like pearls of wisdom
As I emit the smell of *tuak*
The sharpness of its scent
Names slip between stones
Corpses mummify
In clefts of time. Metal flowers
Black buffaloes
Skeletal remains:
A crucifix on every door

Emitting the smell of *tuak*
On following evenings
Was like righting a ladder to the sky
I saw in the air
A rain of beads
Festively woven
A parade of clouds
A herd of wild boars
Smoke from grilled meat
Pouring out from the ceremony
Like thousands of flaming spears
Escorting thousands of souls
To their thrones. Small gateways
Odd weapons
Wooden statues
Coffee beans

On my watch
I followed the seconds and minutes
Spanning the silent distance
Night was then complete
From the shoulder of the hill the moon rose
Then the stars scattered around
And the entire sky reddened
With blood. Death is a party
One's passing is a dance
While loss
Is a song. Silent prayers
Muted mantras
Amid the silence of the universe
Dawn resembles a different face of heaven

Night in Toraja

Shadowy figures flash by
Between green water and fog's foliage.
The moon on the river's surface
A glowing sapphire
On your eyelids. The sky descends
The earth exposes graves
Opening a direct passage
To the ancestors. Years come
Centuries go
Gathering skulls
And arrack bottles

Leaves wave
Far into the crook of silence
Fireflies on the hillside
Are a scattering of beads
From heaven. Pictures of animals
Foot tracks, hand prints
Wooden carvings, stone effigies
Dammar sap and aromatics
From the forest. Clouds form the shape of a cross
The cold chants mysterious mantras
To coffins and cave entrances:
Upright buffaloes
Boars on the ground

Eternity is stored
In rice barns
Supported by pillars of time
A golden fog and shadowy figures
Clusters of clouds and remnants of light
Chase after one another like smoke
And fire. How grand and strange
How festive and solemn
The dances and songs
Seconds fall
To the lap of dawn. A harsh wind
Fills the air with coffee powder
The scent of grilled meats and colorful cakes
From one offering to the other

Dawn is the scattering of beads
From heaven

On Southern Waves

A fickle wind
Off the sea
Brushes your curly hair
Grains of sand
Scatter in the air
Like fog attempting
To disperse

With dusk's passing
The sun retires
Its fine threads
Strike your face

There is color
On your cheeks
A glint of copper
Between your lips

I scrape salt
On the concave
Penninsula. Your shoulders
Twist and turn
Moving up and down

There are jellyfish
In your breasts
A forest preserve
Beneath your navel

I row my boat
Through the wild
Southern waves. I hear you
Release a sigh
A loud current

There is a cave
In your forest
A wild animal
Deep in your heart

From the boat's
Rocking stern
I throw my anchor
Your voice is now
Just a moan
Just a sigh

There is a song
In your roar
A wet corner
Occupied by longing

The southeasterly
Herds your breath
To the crest of age. Scattered stones
Become dust in the air

There is silence
On your tongue's tip
A small dagger
To rip the mosquito net

I follow the wave's rhythm
To the deep
Trough. Your waist
Waves
And sways

There is silence
In your closed eyes
The trace of a smile
Concealed by time

With evening's approach
The sun disappears
Like a door
Quietly closing

A lantern
Slowly dimming

I Want to Be With You

I want to be with you when you go home tonight
To take the city bus and to be crushed together with you inside
I want to be with you at the next stop
And then a kilometer more, where you disembark at the police station
To wait for the next mini-bus. I want be with you, arms scrunched
Inside the stuffy van, as we go past several intersections
Cross over so many railroad tracks, go under overpasses
Pass through tunnels until we are caught in a jam
Near the terminal. I want to be with you when you sigh deeply
Take out a tissue to lap the sweat on your forehead and neck

I want to be with you when you emerge from that ramshackle vehicle
Walk alongside to the motorbike-taxi stand. I want to be with you
As you traverse the potholed path, cut through winding alleyways
To the place you rent with the front ground filled with laundry racks
I want to be with you when you open the door, go into your room
Take off your shoes, remove your clothes and throw them
Beside the couch. I want to be with you when you turn on the fan
Then take a swallow of cold water. I want to be with you
When you turn on the television, smoke a joint, and watch a blue film
I want to be with you when you fiddle with the silence in your room

My Poems

I go to the window to look outside and see a lane
Chock-a-block with drying racks. Pedicabs and vegetable sellers pass by
Time drifts like the almost inaudible news reports coming from
The television at the cigarette stall. At the street corner
People are dancing. The sun is making its way westward
And the air is hot and full of dust
I remember a poem that spoke of
The meaning of freedom. I recall the name
Of a long-forgotten poet. I race to the road
Follow the sidewalk, stop at the market and terminal, and pick up
The remains of the trash and debris of development

My poems rarely speak to park-sweeps, railway-crossing guards
City bus conductors or motorbike taxi drivers. In fact, they've never
Helped jobless people or beggars put their kids through school
My poems, like the government, often forget to ask
Why babies can be disposed of in trash bins, why human bodies
Can be flayed like rabbits, why there are floods and earthquakes
Why thugs can become district leaders, businessmen,
   and government ministers
And why there are so many loud-mouthed preachers on television
Like the bureaucracy, my poems are muddled
and difficult to comprehend
God forbid, my poems are like parliamentarians,
only thinking of themselves.

I suddenly think of a popular *dangdut* song about human rights
And the sexy singer who made it popular. When I go to the window again

I see swathes of hovels being bulldozed and
a warren of houses being torn down
Children are crying, mothers are screaming, and
       gangs of young men
Are throwing rocks at the security forces. Time seems to oscillate
The wind blows harshly as the sun lowers its evening curtain
The red sky resembles the faces of those who have been robbed
The angry look of those who have been looted
A roadside barber sleeps soundly in the shade of a banyan tree
Twilight makes its way towards night, streetlights glow
Silence settles outside the ward office

My poems sometimes forget to say hello
To street vendors, tire repairmen, and used-goods collectors
No, not once have my poems accompanied farmers
When purchasing medicine at the drugstore
Or coolies when paying their bills at the hospital
My poems, like political parties, are averse to ask
Why so many people live in hardship
Why prices rise inexorably, why kerosene is a scarce item
Why rice must be imported from neighboring countries
Why paddy fields are turned into factories
Why forest fires are not being extinguished
Why a hot mud flow is allowed to wreak havoc
My poems, like elections, are not, of course, an answer

Lessons from the Gulf

The elegance of waves
In their fluid dance
The patience of coral
Willingly accepting every blow

The steadfastness of the horizon
As the border between space and time
The maturity of the sun
Willing to drown in order to rise again

A Part of Joy

1

It's been quite a while since I passed the road behind the stadium
The madrasah that was going up right in front of your place
Is finished now. I remember the banyan tree, the one standing
So tall and proud between the kindergarten and guard post
Where I usually stopped to take a leak behind its dangling air roots
After taking you home. The silence was always so eerie when we passed:
Even now I'm feeling the need for some kind of fortifying drink
But the *jamu* stall we used to frequent is no longer there

2

I still own the VW van that looks like a bread-box
But now it's stored in the garage. Even though I could get a good price
I don't want to sell because stored in its body that's started to rust
Are the hundreds of evenings we spent together.
Still sticking to its tattered seat are thousands of hugs and kisses
I still haven't given it the new paint job it needs
And I remember how you once wanted me to paint it green
"To make it look like an army uniform," you suggested
But in the end, the van, which was eight years older than you
And thirteen years younger than me, I painted black
I have to warm its engine often to make sure it will start
And sometimes I take it out for a drive because I still like it very much
Even if it does make me mad, driving me to despair
The rear-view mirror still holds images of the winding path
We followed and on its wheels are figures indicating
The number of kilometers we traveled together

3

Does the city-square still mean anything to you
Where you'd invite me to find a place to sit in one of its corners?
Did you like the sound of the fountain or watching couples
Embrace in pools of darkness not illuminated by park lights
Or being part of the city's VW Club whose members hung out there
Until late at night? So, what is the meaning of joy for you?
You only smiled when I pointed out the position of a star
Appearing by itself in the night sky
Or when I said that the water's rippling sound
Was that of the voice inside my heart

4

Suddenly, I think of you when hearing the clack-clacking sound
Of the noodle vendor as he seeks customers
Again I extract from my memory the name of the street
The walls full of graffiti, the three sharp turns
Causing our stomachs to heave when going 'round them late at night
On the way to the place you rented at the end of the lane
You again stir my loneliness in the fragrance of your hair
The residue of power and the quick kisses you'd sometimes give me
Between the constant patter of the rain, but don't call me now
I can't bear to hear the sound of your voice anymore

5

Time circles like the street around the stadium
Starting from one quiet point and ending
At that same point again. Starting from emptiness, returning
To emptiness. Now, with my distended stomach
And my aching back, I try to run each evening
Try to keep up with people who diligently watch their bodies and health
But I'm no longer as young as I was

Even though you always said love has nothing to do with age
I run slowly, passing by the spot where hawkers sell their goods
Skirting coffee stalls that nightly change their transactional location
Past school-age children playing basketball, past a long row of parked cycles
And young women in tight clothing and brown tinted hair
The silence, too, continues to circle, like people active in sports
People who are afraid of death, like all the scattered posters
With faces of mayoral candidates whose smiles are uniform
Like lines of poetry I never chanced to write. In front of a lane
I sometimes stop, discovering tears running down my cheek

The Prayers of a Flower Farmer

Blessed be the night shortening the distance
To morning mass. Give me a lively orchestra
So as to end this performance of silence, to smell
The early fragrance of the new season's peonies

Blessed be the season anointing the soil
With the sacrament of rain. Give me an allegro of thanks
Its joy flowing from notes on the score sheet
With buds blooming and blossoming before Easter's arrival

Blessed be Easter giving benediction to fallen leaves
With the song of psalms. Give me a lengthy requiem
So that all sorrow fades and the magnolia roots
Once again restore light to the faces of flowers

Northern Ode

Your eyebrows etch the curve of a darkened shoreline
White crests resemble the lapping of tongue tips
In a blue mouth. When a band of gray clouds scatter
In uncertain direction, your forehead reflects the sky's aspect
The row of hills is a string of haunted train cars
Winding around the edge of the shore. Coconut fronds
Wave their hands in the spaces of your green hair
While the sun spreads a golden glow on your skin

Only the wind is able to roam your body's curves,
Your beauty. Only the cold can enter
Your silken robe while plucking the frangipani buds beneath

When in the north the band of clouds again erect
Their tents, evening peeks from behind pandanus sheaths
The sky lowering with the coming of high tide

Climbing the Hill of Prayer

Love is the wooden beam
I shoulder from the valley
To the hilltop. Drops of blood
On the cracked soil,
Chips of limestone
Mark the trail of this final exile

But remembrance of troubled thoughts
And weary feelings pass. Time seems to evanesce
Memory vanishes, the prayers I drag behind me
Snagged on lines of prophecy
I imagine a heaven
Abrim with parody

Love is the number of wounds,
The pain I still feel
In my chest and side. Nothing has changed
But night which is now allied with silence
You and I recreated,
Released to roam to earth

History only notes the scenes
Happening outside ourselves. The ink is dry
The pen is broken and the prayers that I rolled out
Tripped on a pile of stones
Arranged by a monk
To resemble my physiognomy

Coconut Tart

I open the window and the mist outside looks like
Finely grated cheese. With muteness as the background
For this unexpected meeting of ours, the clock seemed to lose
   its tock
Christmas Eve became a brief episode for the purging of wounds

Tomorrow morning you must leave. I must go as well
To finish out the rest of the year in places not to be found
On maps. The piece of coconut tart I gave you
A monument to commemorate sweet longing

When the mist turned into rain I fetched my camera
To capture in photographs for eternity those falling drops,
Imagining the rain having its source in your eyes

There are no words I can say to you; I have only a smile
And a piece of coconut tart. There are no words
Silence is the language that time most understands

An Episode Repeated

Time is like shards of crystal falling on asphalt
I thought, as evening began to descend
A set of blue lights flashed between Christmas trees
Behind them, dim bulbs lit a row of cafes

The sound of the choir behind the cathedral walls seemed sad
The air's temperature translated itself into part of a proverb
I walked alone along the sidewalk and the cobblestone piazza
Crossing the bridge, passing stop lights, corners of the past

Coming back I found the crystal shards on the steps of an old castle
Remembering a small island not to be found on maps
I quickly put on a thick jacket and rushed to the bus stop

At night's end something stealthily sounded the trumpet
Of separation. My eyes narrowed like tunnels
Quivering to see a pair of blue lights through the murk

After the Drizzle

You might still recall that after the drizzle that morning
The leaves on the laurel tree appeared brighter than usual
 Perhaps you've not forgotten that after that first peck on the cheek
The air at the city's edge took on greater freshness

When you smiled your face was like the horizon at twilight
A deep red glow lacquered by gloaming
When you nodded your eyelashes looked like ficus fronds
Dangling leaves concealing tombstones below

Smiling and nodding are but a small part of beauty
Often displayed by mountain cliffs in the south,
The surface of the earth burying true beauty

The curve of brows and lashes resembling fronds
Might appear as a painting in a vision of the world
But the true painting is hidden behind the walls of your heart

Galunggung's Message

I follow the fog's vague trail between rows of pines
Their needles scattered about the ground
Dew drops still cling to the bark of trees
The afternoon feels odd. Galunggung an open book

The walls forming the mountain's cone
Say that magma is the yearning it holds
Which time continues to store. Looking down,
The grren lake emerges within a ring of white sulfur

Here I hope to study the gentle way fog moves
Without disturbance, learning the mountain's ability
To store and tend to its longing for years on end

I hope to study the patience of magma knowing when
To speak, learning from honest yearning
That even when repressed does not rebel

I Thought

I thought rain had formed pools in your eyes
But it was your sadness that caused clouds to cluster
And to morph into tears. I am amazed by twilight
Its play of gradations between subdued and bright

I thought lighting had infused your song
But it was your voice that echoed in the air
As a statement of love. Twilight truly astounds me
Its ability to create such a harmonious composition

I thought the wind had stirred your desire
But it was your breath that controlled the storm in the sea
Causing high and low tides to occur. Once again I thought
Twilight was behind the dimmed light of dusk

I thought fog had calmed your mind
But it was your longing that silenced the universe
At twilight's end. I thought that the scarlet sky
Was an event uniting all colors in your heart

Talisé Shore

My steps feel heavy as I descend the footpath
Turning my head aside, I brush away the high grass
As if passing memories. I then catch a different scent
An unusual aroma blown by the waves into the air

I come to this shore not to continue the hostility
The mantra I'd been chanting merely means to warm my lungs
For some time now I've been mute, forgetting how to speak
Your name. For some time I've been trapped in the rubble of time

My fingers pluck silence from the horizonless expanse
Strings vibrate in a vacuum broken by the wind
Islands become a smattering of ever smaller dots

For some time I've waited for your voice to come down to find me
On earth. For some time I've imagined that miraculous encounter
When Your word and thunder meld, salt with the sea

In the Direction of Donggala

Alone I walk, following the footpath up the hill
Pine trees appear as symbols planted by time
On battered bark, I see something written
My name and yours. You once carved them there

Long you have gone becoming an echo of loss
The echo of a poem staggering in its attempt to traverse
Rivers and forests. To the end of remembrance, I sought you
Concealing yourself amid a cluster of symbols

Alone I walk, following the footpath on that hill
Awareness is the tree where sap is constantly tapped
There is a picture of a heart and our names. I carved it

Near the cliff's edge I see the horizon but not as a poem
It has changed to an unending wilderness of sentences
Having lost your trail by forgetting to read the signals

Sulamadaha

Fog's obscure trail leads toward the atoll
Between the sound of slowly-beating waves
An apron of sand meanders to the end of the cove
Creating a blue curve licking the white foam

Like a promontory with hollows in its sheer wall
A painting to forever be interpreted through the cycles of time
Each interpretation giving birth to a range of other meanings
Unaware of who among us widens that distance of longing

We will study from the sea that stores gentle symbols
In the ferocity of its waves. We will take lessons from the mountain
Open to the comings and goings of birds

Let our convictions discover their own horizon, my love
Just as every boat must sail to its individual destiny
We will meet at the time the moon and sun touch

Tapulaga

My footsteps end at a pier which is thrusting itself
Into the cove. There are no words to describe
Loss as being another form of surrender
Wood pylons only indicate where I must stand

An island appears to be an abandoned ship midsea
Cottages floating among the stillness and solitude
The silent tracks you left form an extended ripple
Vanishing in the distance. Your voice is stored in the waves

I try to remember you at a spannable distance
One strait after another never led us anywhere
The heart being the final destination of all the world's way stations

The writing on the sand is an artifact of our love
A tale etched in the air soon expunged by weather
The meeting between sky and earth is forever delayed

There Are No More Twilights

There are no more twilights speaking to me
In pastel colors. The air is still blanketed with fog
While cloud clusters, like submarines
Slowly circle all the corners of
This old town. I see the sides of the canals
Marble bridges and steel piles
All of them black. Black are the trunks of old lindens too
Standing amid the corpses of leaves yet to be raked
Black-veiled women are strolling about
The sidewalks seem filled with hundreds of bats
Store windows full with black overcoats
Black dresses. I haven't found your tombstone
Cafés and restaurants begin to turn on
Their dim lights. I order a glass of coffee
As I want to swallow the warmth of waiting

There are no more twilights speaking to me
In pastel colors. Bus stops are drenched with rain
Stations become monuments to transience
As trains come and go; hungry people hug themselves
In the cold
There's something I want to write in the pages of your diary
About the many years of your long and hard flight,
The silent seconds that froze,
The lonely minutes suddenly stopping
At the end of your veins. I have walked down many paths
Running from lane to lane, swimming from canal to canal,

Entering painting galleries, watching porno films,
Laughing while cursing my age crawling
On the stairs of time. I take a swig on a bottle of beer
Wanting to savor the harsh taste of longing

There are no more twilights speaking to me
In pastel colors. The snow I have long been waiting for
Sends only its temperament through gusts of wind
A stiff disposition, one cold and threatening
Gardens are still black, their soil wet and black
On the roadside I see sharp linden branches
Shaped like your small lips in solemn prayer during a storm
Or like your short sentences caught in the throat
As the sky grows lower the cathedral towers cut through
Cloud clusters. In the distance lights are dim
Letters jump, leaving the large trees behind
Like bats. I have yet to find your tombstone
Only imagining the cotton snow falling
On your grave. I go to my hotel and take a hit of weed
I still want to roam in the wilderness of words

Impressions of Liu Sanjie

1

A wooden sampan moves calmly
From a barely visible point. The air is fresh
Fog covers the river's clear water
As twilight slowly descends, a light drizzle falls

2

A line of buffalo leaves the rice fields
Between the river and the scattered, stony hills
A scarlet light shines softly from behind the fog
The wooden sampan becoming a sign of silence

3

The evening wind may have been sent
From a distant land. Its woosh begets movement
A dancer flies lightly, following the river's course
Her thin body twisting about like a falling leaf

4

The audible night music permeates from a well
In the woods. Rustling leaves, chirping birds, buzzing insects
The poetry reflecting off the water's surface
Light congeals as spaces fill with darkness

5

The river's language is the breath of a past civilization
Its slow course drags with it anything that floats
A wooden sampan moves slowly from century to century
A voyage without a map and going nowhere

6

A third of the night has passed, lanterns still flicker
On top of a hill a dancer lets go of her own body
Piece after piece of clothing flying away like wingless words
A verse of poetry failing to infuse passion

Reading the Signs

At the river's mouth I vaguely hear the approach of time's footsteps
The stand of mangroves on the shore becomes an echo chamber
When the dry season wind plays catch with the rolling waves
I am left far outside the limits of transience

Though all that is visible before us now is only fog
Surely there are things yet to be discovered. In reading the signs
Thinking of how the sky lowers and the earth rises
I do not attempt to squeeze water from a stone

A journey is the seconds flowing from the mountain
And taken by the river to its mouth. Understanding is but
Fine grains of sand making their way to the middle of the sea

Slowly I witness as twilight transforms into a stage
A recital of colors being performed on the horizon
In the distance a cluster of islands flutter like backup dancers

Crossing to Bokori

On the uninhabited island I hear soft music
The stretch of sand a musical score from which time flows
Silvery crests chase the gentle and greenish waves
I cross to the territorial border of longing

Though only palms and pines shade me
I feel the beauty of the morning. Fishes sing
Seagulls dance while clouds form a composition
I imagine everything to be a silent orchestra

The distance between us is just a strait's width
Inhabited by coral flowers. Long have I looked into the watery
	mirror
Explored its depths as if entering your heart's cave

The crashing of waves on my back
The feel of the reef on my heels becomes an expression
Which I can only interpret when we are far apart

Sagaraanakan

I see the light's end behind the haze
A star falls, drowning in the river's mouth
The boats sailing on the water disappear
Behind the island. A splash of ink stains the sea

I enter the fissure between the two large coral mounds
Squeezing into the mesh made of aerial roots from ficus trees
Evening has become the point that cannot be touched
By words. My eyes dim with the twilight

Where is the footpath that directed my childhood
To the well? Each and every journey gives birth
To possibilities difficult to picture again

Where is the love song in which I was prophesized
To turn to stone? Caves seem to conceal the past
My meditation another journey outside of time

Nusakambangan

I stare in the distance, to the far side of the cape
From the cliff, fishermen's boats
Seem like fireflies. A village is visible
Its floating homes made of bamboo

Cotton clouds sail by beneath an orange sky
Seagulls fly in no certain direction
Where must my thoughts roam
Imagining the sun's imminent merging with the sea

Around me are the aerial roots of an old banyan
A ravine with a gaping mouth between two hills
The waves' surface absorbing the colors of the sky

Fading dusk ebbs at the moment fog places its feet
On the water. From the cliff top I see the fishermen's boats
Fireflies isolating themselves one from the other

Amazing

As with your footprints in the sand, your words
Were erased, the prophecy you wrote there, gone
As the waves recede, their blows grow faint in sound
And, suddenly, the shore is silent. The sea: a secret longing
Not easily translated into words

Gradually, before the westerly resends its sign
I forget your vanished words. The firmament
Is now a curved line with a cluster of clouds below
I see no longer seagulls slicing through the gloom
Twilight is the answer to my every surprise

I Welcome the Sun

I fell asleep hugging an ebony tree
And dreamt of a beautiful valley
Colored with wild flowers. A flowing river
Whose rippling water is background music
For birds' and insects' songs

I hear what the wind is saying
Make note of all the sun conveys
To me. In the shade of the ebony
I witness the luxuriant end to evening
As colors condense and grow radiant

I fell asleep hugging that tree, my love,
Imagined it to be a wooden stage
With a thatched roof. And I, naked, at dawn
Welcoming the sun rising over the hilltop
As you immersed yourself in the well

Nipah Bay

You go home before the call to prayer
Resounds in the direction of the prayer house
Before a troop of clouds in the western sky
Turn into calligraphy. And before bats
Leave their silent roosts

You go home before the fishermen
Lift their anchors. Before dots of fire
Proliferate, like fireflies, out at sea
Before the hands of your wristwatch
Remind you that time is running out

You go home before the two islets
In the channel, silently grow closer
Before the two opposing shores
Wave their hands once before. Before the old poet
Relates his tale of one loss after another

About A Poet

Slowly, towards sunrise, dawn approaches
The walls of the wharf. Boats begin to dock
The reddish horizon loosens her hair
And the air brushes her mane with its gusts

At the bay's end, a cloud-cloaked sun emerges
Whose shafts of light are reflected on the sea's surface
A poet sets out to sea, then vanishes behind the waves
But time does not call his disappearance a loss

One Step from your Heart

In the sand are your footprints
But the message you wrote, illegible
Without the raging waves, the coast is still
The sea is a secret, not easily revealed
When every word melds with the weather

One step from your heart, I stop momentarily
To listen to the sound of bells still ringing
In the air. In the distance, the horizon curves
A seagull cuts through the gloaming
And colors condense in my eyes

The Language of Longing

With the bottles of wine I drank
That cold night, I was burnt by the glow
Of lantern light. I watched you writhe
In a prolonged outburst of anxiousness
Your hands twirling, as if stirring
A slick and slithery wind. Music is but background
For events—like air kisses in times of parting

When waves strike the pier's pillars
Radiant droplets spread across the shore
Roads curve and come to an end at a lane
Where all of this began. Clouds mimic
The gentle sway of your floating body
Bottles shrink, absorbed by time. And music
Like a kiss, becomes the language of longing

Monument to Resolution

Reflecting on the sea's spume that erodes the coral
Is much like looking back at days past
Of an old calendar. The waves' pounding seems sluggish
Twilight sheds its pink light on the unknown
Which I chase with leaden footsteps

Wiping away the droplets that wet my cheeks
Is like reopening the pages in a book of forgotten
Prophecies. Heaven and earth will always be apart
Loss after loss will always repeat itself
Which I deem to be a monument to resolution

Come Low Tide

Come low tide, and beneath the sky
Where dawn's light spreads, your tears sparkle
With the rolling of waves. Silently staring in the sea's mirror
I see your sadness to be humus for the hard-soiled hills
Where the grasses and plants that manage to grow
Are words which write their own stories

The curved and cliff-lined cape is not just a respite
For the roaring headwind. Indeed, the horizon's expanse
Is no barrier for distinct interpretations
From other directions. Beneath the lightening sky
I see your tears turn into crimson pendants
Which, with the waves, slowly spray the land

Twilight's Tongue

When twilight sticks out its orange tongue
It turns into a footpath which stretches
To the horizon. Scattered gray clouds
Make gaps for shafts of light
Now fading with the dimming of the sun

The stars that later appear
Seem to plunge the gleam in your eyes
To the bottom of the sea. I see the waves
Constantly pounding in your chest
As a sign of never-ending restlessness

Night climbs the hill until dawn
The footpath, ending at the edge the cliff
Is now shrouded in fog. I search
But cannot find your eyes in the silence
While the morning call to prayer has yet to resound

Self-talk 1

Though the cogon grass grows higher and the moon
Grows dimmer in my heart, I will never forget you
My love. I continue to go forward
Entering rooms I'd once visited long before,
A maze that leads me to no certain
Destination. I want to seek myself in you

I continue going forward. Ignoring all signs
On the roads that crisscross before me
The moon descends, then disappears
Behind clouds. I walk through the fog
Prodded forward by the air waves at my back
To the limits. I want to insert you inside me

Self-talk 2

It's grueling to spend late nights without you
A constant struggle in my heart
At whose end, I cry yet also hoot
In laughter at myself. A shooting star
Whose light sears the mountain tops
While, at the same time, hot clouds envelop me

I neither saw the signs, nor understood
The hot lava in the riverbed to be your prophecy
I was unable to translate the forest fire
Into a Word. Near sunrise, I continued walking
Dawn's glimmer becoming a vast purple canvas
And when slowly saying your name, I forgot myself

Self-talk 3

Beneath dawn's light, I walk, my love
Viewing each step as a tick of the clock
Speaking your name, with my eyes closed. In my heart
The chanting of insects disturbs the silence
With my every step, I come closer to dawn
To welcome the sun rising from its hermitage

I keep walking. In silence
The air growing cooler, my body covered in dew
Having given up my hunt for the Word, because words
Turn into the air inside my chest. And the horizon
Forever being empty sheets of paper
On which I write poems of your existence and nonexistence

Self-talk 4

Every parting is a repeat of a time of drought
The wind blows me far into the stillness of time
To the vast expanse of a desert with no end
I call out for no one, proceeding alone
In the face of storms and typhoons. All alone
As clouds descend ever closer to earth

My mind is in constant turmoil, my heart busy
With questions. But I entrust my footsteps to my feet
Nature makes me aware of the way of seasons
When an escarpment begins to rise and surround me
And the darkening red sky appears ready to fall on me
I do not call out for anyone. I walk on alone

Self-talk 5

I sail, pushed by the gusting wind, my love
Traversing the waves of your briny body
Passing between symbol-laden coral krantzes
From the look in your eyes, I get an inkling
of the ocean's depth and its secrets. I sail
Without a boat, through slowly-unfolding time

When dawn tethers my prayers to the shore
A long tunnel appears before me
Again, I drag my feet as I go towards its end
That being the limits of surrender. I take in the air
I shield my words so that they burn like a lamp
And illuminate my journey of self understanding

Self-talk 6

The words I breathe intoxicate me
For years I went forward, without turning
Without looking back. I looked for you in the dark
But found only myself, stranded there
Amid sparkling light, I could see nothing
And could no longer hear strange, outside voices

I have visited nameless mosques
Abandoned churches, and emptied
Monasteries. I have prayed most everywhere
The highway being an endless prayer mat
A series of mercury lamps are little candles.
My offering. Once again, I utter your name

About Schedules

The sound of the wind
Blowing
From the river's direction

Cold air
A sour smell
An early dry season

Leaves fall
Dry twigs break
Day comes slowly

Before us
A bird flies
Ever lower

A bird
A lost sea gull
Perhaps

As day descends
I see the horizon
In the gloaming

A blurred horizon
An uncertain marker
A symbol for what's to come

We proceed
To the port
Where death is

Waiting. Then
We talk to time
About schedules

You are leaving
But I must go back
Into myself

With the sound of the waves
Striking the dock
Their foam sizzles

The distance between us
Is created by the space
Between silent paragraphs

The distance between us
Reflects its echo
In metaphors

And death
Becomes enchanting
In the secrecy of words

One Morning at Karet Bivac Cemetery

That morning
I didn't ask
How old
Is love

But the dew replied
By flooding my eyes
And dripping something
On my cheek

That morning
I did remember you
As an adult
In terms of time

A senior
In the knowledge of longing
The sting and pain
Of a life in poetry

That morning
I made a pilgrimage
I read your poem
On a stone

From the Window of Le Meridien

Drawing back the curtains
In a room on the ninth floor
I seem to be able to see you
In the glimmer and glare of this city

Lights flash
On tall buildings
When, bare-chested
You throw your fist in the air

In the early hours
Words continued to fall
On emptied streets

In the early hours
You rigidly remained at the window
Facing the world, alone

Past Cibatu Station

At the end of the curving rail
Or the limits of vision:
Love is, in fact, blind

In the waiting room
As passengers rush to board
Or disembark. You sit alone

The train will soon depart again
The rails slowly begin to creak
A whistle blows. Utter quiet

That night, I hoped
To welcome you. But was unable
To look through the window
While passing by

Continuing westward
To the end of the curving rails
To the limits of vision:

Love is, in fact, blind. What's there to say?
Some come, some go
Some realize nothing at all

Glossary of Names and Geographical Locations

Aceh	The westernmost province of Indonesia located on the northern end of Sumatra with Banda Aceh being its capital and largest city. Granted a special autonomous status, Aceh is a religiously conservative territory and the only Indonesian province practicing Sharia law officially.
Anne	"Anne" (in the poem "Chant") refers to Anne Rufaidah, a former classmate of the poet in the Faculty of Art and Design at the Bandung Institute of Technology. By wearing a *jilbab*, she became a symbol of protest against the government when the wearing of scarves in schools was banned by the Department of Education and Culture in the early 1980s. She went on to become a pioneer of Muslim fashion in Indonesia.
Arco Etrusco	Also known as the Arch of Augustus, the Etruscan Arch is one of eight gates in the Etruscan wall of Perugia. It was constructed in the second half of the 3rd century BC. The arch is part of a massive set of walls which are 9.1 m tall and 2,900 m long made of travertine and set without mortar.
Attar	Abu Hamid bin Abu Bakr Ibrahim (1145–1221), better known by his pen-names Farīd ud-Dīn and Attar was a Persian poet, theoretician of Sufism, and hagiographer from Nishapur who had an immense and lasting influence on Persian poetry and Sufism.
Bagolo	A village in the regency of Pangandaran on the southern coast of Java.

Basra	An Iraqi city located on the Shatt al-Arab. It is also Iraq's main port, although it does not have deep water access. In the 740s, Basra became an intellectual center and home to the elite Basra School of Grammar.
Bilal	Bilal ibn Rabah (580–640 AD) was one of the most trusted and loyal companions of Muhammad. Born in Mecca, he was a former slave who became famous for his beautiful voice with which he called people to their prayers.
Bokori	An island in Southeast Sulawesi once known for its beauty but almost lost now due to abrasion.
Cipasung	The name of both a village near Tasikmalaya, West Java, and a religious boarding school established and run by the family of Acep Zamzam Noor.
Daud	Mulla Daud was the first poet in the ideology of Sufism. He wrote in early Hindi in the 14th century.
Dini	"Dini" (in the poem "The Mountain's Breath") refers to Nur Islami Dini, a jilbab-wearing woman from Tasikmalaya.
Donggala	A regency in the province of Central Sulawesi, Indonesia whose capital is Banawa, located 34 km north from Palu, capital of the province. In September 2018, Donggala and Palu suffered heavy casualties due to a tsunami.
Galunggung	Mount Galunggung is an active stratovolcano in West Java, around 80 km southeast of the West Java provincial capital, Bandung. Galunggung had its first historical eruption in 1500. More recently, the volcano erupted again in 1982.
Hafiz	The pen name for Khwāja Shams-ud-Dīn Muḥammad Ḥāfeẓ-e Shīrāzī (1315-1390), a Persian poet who lauded the joys of love and wine but also targeted religious hypocrisy. His work is regarded by some as a pinnacle of Persian literature. His pen name means "the memorizer" or "the safekeeper."

Hamzah	Hamzah ibn Abd al-Muttalib (570–625) was a foster brother, companion, and paternal uncle of the prophet Muhammad who was killed in the Battle of Uhud on 22 March 625.
Imana Tahira	The poet's daughter, also a published poet.
Inne Ratu	Inne Ratu (in the poem "Socccer") was a close friend of the author when he was a student at ITB.
Jalaluddin	Jalal ad-Din Muhammad Rumi (1207–1273), also named *Mawlānā*, which means *Our Master*, is one of the Islamic world's greatest poets. A Sufi mystic, philosopher, and lover of humanity, he is usually known in the English-speaking world simply as Rumi.
Jami	Nūr ad-Dīn 'Abd ar-Rahmān Jāmī also known as Mawlanā Nūr al-Dīn 'Abd al-Rahmān or Abd-Al-Rahmān Nur-Al-Din Muhammad Dashti, or simply as Jami or Djāmī and in Turkey as Molla Cami (1414–1492), was a Persian Sunni poet who is known for his achievements as a prolific scholar and writer of mystical Sufi literature.
Karang Setra	An entertainment complex in Bandung, West Java, with a hotel and waterpark.
Kumbasari	A market in Denpasar, Bali.
Lhok Nga	The name of a town and region on the Pacific side of the province of Aceh. In 2004 the town completely destroyed by the Boxing Day Tsunami and its population dwindled from 7,500 to 400.
Lina Sagaral Reyes	Lina Sagaral Reyes is an author and journalist based in Mindanao, Philippines. Her main abiding interest has been in writing non-fiction on gender and development issues.
Liu Sanjie	A Chinese folk music singer, the earliest story about whom can be found in the Southern Song Dynasty (1127-1279). She was said to be a wunderkind, able to compose impromptu songs at will.
Londa	The site of Torajan cave tombs in Central Sulawesi.

Malika Hamoudi	Malika Hamoudi refers to a friend of the poet, a French woman of Algerian descent who toured museums in Paris with the poet in 1996.
Malioboro	A major shopping street in Yogyakarta. The name is also used more generally for the neighborhood around the street.
Marilyn Monroe	Marilyn Monroe (1926–1962) was an American actress, model, and singer who became one of the most popular sex symbols of the 1950s and early 1960s.
Marwa	Marwa is one of two small hills now located in the Great Mosque of Mecca, Saudi Arabia. (The other is Safa.) Muslims travel back and forth between them seven times, during the ritual pilgrimages of hajj and umrah.
Mecca	Mecca, in western Saudi Arabia, is Islam's holiest city, as it's the birthplace of the Prophet Muhammad and the faith itself. Only Muslims are allowed in the city.
Melva	"Melva" (in the poem "A Poet Once More") is the name of a woman the author knew in Bandung who worked in sales but had ambitions of becoming a dangdut singer.
Mina	Mina is a neighborhood of Mecca situated 5 kilometers to the east of the city. It stands on the road from Mecca's city centre to the Hill of Arafat and is the site where tents for pilgrims are erected during the pilgrimage seasons.
Montmartre	Montmartre is a large hill in Paris. It is 130 m (430 ft) high and gives its name to the surrounding district. Montmartre is primarily known for its artistic history.
Nusakambangan	Variation on "Nusa Kambangan," an island off the southern coast of Java in the Cilacap regency. The island has the status of a nature preserve but is better known as the location of several high-security penitentiaries located there.

| Paesaggio | Italian for "landscape" or scenery. |

Paesaggio — Italian for "landscape" or scenery.

Pangrango — A dormant stratovolcano located in the Sunda Arc of West Java. It is located about 80 km south of Jakarta and has a height of 3,019 meters.

Rabi'a — Rābi'a al-'Adawiyya al-Qaysiyya was a Muslim saint and Sufi mystic said to have been born between 714 and 718 CE in Basra, Iraq. She is known in some parts of the world as, Hazrat Bibi Rabia Basri, Rabia Al Basri or simply Rabia Basri

Safa — Safa is one of two small hills now located in the Great Mosque of Mecca, Saudi Arabia. (The other is Marwa.) Muslims travel back and forth between them seven times, during the ritual pilgrimages of hajj and umrah.

Sana'i — Hakim Abul-Majd Majdūd ibn Ādam Sanā'ī Ghaznavi, more commonly known as Sanai, was a Persian poet from Ghazni who lived his life in Ghazni at the time of its golden age, in medieval Khorassan, which is now located in Afghanistan. He was born in 1080 and died between 1131 and 1141.

Sagaraanakan — Variation of "Segara Anakan," a giant lagoon located on the southern coast of Java on the border between the provinces of West Java and Central Java. It is situated between Java Island and the much smaller island of Nusakambangan in the Cilacap Regency.

Seine — The Seine is a 777-kilometer-long river and an important commercial waterway within the Paris Basin in the north of France.

Sulaiman — "Sulaiman" (in the poem "Lovers"), or "Solomon" in English, refers to the king of Israel who ruled from 970 to 931 BCE. Purported to be able to speak to animals, he is considered by Muslims to be one of the major prophets.

Sulamadaha — Sulamadaha is a famous beach in the subdistrict of West Ternate in the province of North Maluku, Indonesia.

Talisé	Talisé is a subdistrict if the Mantikulore District, located near the city of Palu, in Central Sulawesi. The area is known for the beauty of its shoreline.
Tapulaga	A subdistrict on the coast of Southeast Sulawesi known for its coast line.
Tjut Njak Dien	Tjut Njak Dien, also spelled "Cut Nyak Dhien" or "Tjoet Nja' Dhien" (1848–1908) was a leader of the Acehnese guerrilla forces during the Aceh War with the Dutch. Following the death of her husband Teuku Umar, she led guerrilla actions against the Dutch for 25 years.
Toraja	Toraja (or Tana Toraja in Indonesian) is a regency in the South Sulawesi province of Indonesia and home to the Toraja ethnic group. The area is famous for its ancestor and death rituals.
Trasimeno	Lake Trasimeno (also referred to as Trasimene or Thrasimene in English) is a lake in the the province of Perugia, in the Umbria region of Italy.
Tugu	Name of the central train station in Yogyakarta.
Umbria	A region of central Italy. Lake Trasimeno is located there and the area is known for its landscapes, traditions, history, culinary delights, artistic legacy, and influence on culture.
Yunus	Yunus Emre (1238-1320), a Sufi dervish of Anatolia, is considered by many to be one of the most important Turkish poets. His poetry expresses a deep personal mysticism and humanism and love for God.

Publication Data

Sources

JMR = *Jalan Menuju Rumahmu* (Grasindo, 2004)

ZDD = *Ziarah ke Dalam Diri* (Unpublished MS)

BDK = *Bagian dari Kegembiraan* (Pustaka Azan, 2013)

MPL = *Menjadi Penyair Lagi* (Pustaka Azan, 2007)

BKR = *Berguru Kepada Rindu* (Diva Press, 2017)

PA = *Pastoral* (Unpublished MS)

DAU = *Di Atas Umbria* (Indonesia Tera, 1999)

TO = *Tonggeret* (Diva Press, 2020)

DLK = *Di Luar Kata* (Pustaka Firdaus, 1996)

TPT = *Tulisan pada Tembok* (Komodo Books, 2011)

ML = *Membaca Lambang* (Gramedia, 2018)

TA = *Titik Akanan* (Diva Press, 2023)

English Title	Indonesian Title	Written	Source
Pangrango	Pangrango	1980	JMR
Wind and Rock	Angin dan Batu	1984	JMR
Chant	Zikir	1984	TPT
My Melancholy Blues	My Melancholy Blues	1986	MPL
With the Grass, I Weep	Aku Menangis Bersama Rumput	1987	JMR
Solitude	Solitude	1987	JMR
Melancholia	Melancholia	1987	JMR
The Poet's Earth	Bumi Penyair	1989	JMR
Evening Song	Nyanyian Sore	1989	DLK
Cipasung	Cipasung	1989	DLK
Pastoral	Pastoral	1991	DAU
Lovers	Para Kekasih	1992	JMR

Trasimeno	Trasimeno	1992	DAU
Arco Etrusco	Arco Etrusco	1992	DAU
River and Estuary	Sungai dan Muara	1992	DAU
Above Umbria	Di Atas Umbria	1993	DAU
Paesaggio	Paesaggio	1993	DAU
The Rain Has Died	Hujan Telah Reda	1993-1994	DAU
Kumbasari Market, Denpasar	Pasar Kumbasari	1995	DAU
For Lina Sagaral Reyes	Buat Lina Sagaral Reyes	1996	DAU
Never to Die	Tak Mati-Mati	1996	BDK
A Swatch of Twilight	Sepotong Senja	2006	BDK
Trail *)	Jejak	2006	BDK
A Poet Once More	Menjadi Penyair Lagi	1996	MPL
The Mountain's Breath	Napas Gunung	1997	MPL
A Story for Imana Tahira	Cerita buat Imana Tahira	1996	BDK
For Malika Hamoudi	Buat Malika Hamoudi	1997	DAU
Yet to Come	Belum Singgah	1997-1998	DAU
Age*)	Usia	2002	JMR
Soccer	Sepak Bola	2005	MPL
Secrets *)	Rahasia	2006	MPL
On Malioboro *)	Di Malioboro	2006	MPL
Love's Force *)	Kekuasaan	2006	BDK
Like Death Approaching *)	Seperti Ajal yang Datang Tanpa Bicara	2006	BDK
Like Love and Death	Seperti Cinta dan Maut	2006	BDK

*)An asterisk indicates that an earlier version of the translation was first published in *Like Death Approaching & Other Poems* (Jakarta: Lontar, 2015).

Pilgrimage to Londa	Ziarah ke Londa	2007	ML
Night in Toraja	Malam di Toraja	2007	ML
On Southern Waves	Pada Ombak Selatan	2007	ML
I Want to Be With You	Aku Ingin Menemanimu	2007	BDK
My Poems *)	Puisiku	2009	BDK
Lessons from the Gulf	Pelajaran dari Teluk	2014	BKR
A Part of Joy *)	Bagian dari Kegembiraan	2007	BDK
The Prayers of a Flower Farmer	Doa Petani Bunga	2015	ML
Northern Ode	Madah dari Utara	2015	BKR
Climbing the Hill of Prayer	Mendaki Bukit Doa	2015	ML
Coconut Tart	Klappertart	2015	ML
An Episode Repeated	Episode yang Berulang	2016	ML
After the Drizzle	Sehabis Gerimis	2016	BKR
Galunggung's Message	Amanat Galunggung	2016	BKR
I Thought That Rain	Aku Menduga Hujan	2016	BKR
Talisé Coast	Pantai Talise	2016	ML
In the Direction of Donggala	Arah Donggala	2016	ML
Sulamadaha	Sulamadaha	2016	ML
Tapulaga	Tapulaga	2017	ML
There Are No More Twilights	Tak Ada Lagi Senja	2017	PA
Impressions of Liu Sanjie	Impression Liu Sanjie	2017	PA
Reading the Signs	Membaca Lambang	2017	ML
Crossing to Bokori	Menyeberang ke Bokori	2017	ML
Sagaraanakan	Sagaraanakan	2018	ZDD
Nusakambangan	Nusakambangan	2018	ZDD
Amazing	Ketakjuban	2020	TA
I Welcome the Sun	Menyambut Matahari	2020	TA

Nipah Bay	Teluk Nipah	2020	The Author
About a Poet	Tentang Seorang Penyair	2020	The Author
One Step from your Heart	Selangkah dari Hatimu	2020	The Author
Monument to Resolution	Monumen Ketabahan	2021	The Author
At the Border of Longing	Batas dari Rindu	2021	The Author
Near Low Tide	Menjelang Surut	2021	The Author
Twilight's Tongue	Lidah Senja	2021	The Author
Self-talk 1	Percakapan Diri (1)	2022	TA
Self-talk 2	Percakapan Diri (2)	2022	TA
Self-talk 3	Percakapan Diri (3)	2022	TA
Self-talk 4	Percakapan Diri (4)	2022	TA
Self-talk 5	Percakapan Diri (5)	2022	TA
Self-talk 6	Percakapan Diri (6)	2022	TA
About Schedules	Perihal Jadwal	2023	The Author
One Morning at Karet Bivac Cemetery	Suatu Pagi di Karet Bivak	2024	The Author
From the Window of Le Meridien	Dari Jendela Le Meridien	2024	The Author
Past Cibatu Station	Lewat Stasiun Cibatu	2024	The Author

An Interview with the Poet[*]

ZH: Before asking anything else, I'd like to find out from you how it was that you first began to write poetry in the small town where you grew up.

AZN: I am from Cipasung, West Java, home to Cipasung Pondok Pesantren, the Islamic boarding school my grandfather, KH Ruhiat, established and which was later run by my father, KH Muhammad Ilyas Ruchiat. I lived at our family's home, however, and only went to the pesantren to play.

    I owe the start of my writing career to the abundance of reading materials we had at my home. My mother subscribed to the Sundanese-language magazine, *Manglé*, which led me to first write poetry in Sundanese, and my father subscribed to several Indonesian-language newspapers—*Pelita, Suara Karya,* and *Pikiran Rakyat*—all of which had poetry columns, which is what then led me to write in Indonesian as well. It was my frequent reading of poetry that got me interested in writing poems myself. At the same time, I also credit the intensely lyrical atmosphere of the pesantren in its rural setting.

    As a junior high school student, the only poets I knew

---

[*] This "conversation" with the Acep Zamzam Noor (AZN) is based on an interview conducted by Zen Hae (ZH) on December 7, 2021.

of wer whose books were available at my school, but when I was in senior high school there was a mobile library run by the Tasikmalaya City government that came to my school and the pesantren twice a week. This mobile library had in its collection the many literary titles Pustaka Jaya published. Students were allowed to borrow one book a week for a week at a time and it was then I became familiar with the work of other poets such as Kuntowijoyo, Abdul Hadi WM, Ramadhan KH, Subagio Sastrowardoyo, and Rendra.

ZH: Having begun to read poetry at a relatively young age, what was your view on poetry at that time?

AZN: I can't say what I thought of poetry at that time, not in theoretical terms anyway; I just knew that poetry gave me pleasure—both in reading poems and in writing them.

Writing poetry became the means through which I was able to express my adolescent feelings. I had also begun to teach myself to draw at around that same time and I came to believe that everyone needs a media through which to express their feelings. I found mine in writing and in art. Poetry became for me my road to life, an unplanned route but one I knew I had to follow. Poetry became for me an indispensable part of my life.

As I began to produce my own poems, I read and studied the work of other poets. In time, I established a writers' community of like-minded people, people who wrote poetry. Again, it would be impossible to separate poetry from my life, but that's not how it was at the very beginning; the process was gradual and happened naturally over time.

ZH: After graduating from high school you enrolled at the Faculty of Arts and Design at the Bandung Institute of Technology. Had you already begun to paint?

AZN: Not at that stage. I was still learning to draw.

ZH: The reason I ask is because in many of your poems, visual images dominate, especially ones from the "Above Umbria" period when you were an art student in Italy. Was this a result of your growing involvement in the art world?

AZN: If you are asking if it was a conscious decision on my part, I think not. In both my writing and painting, I've always been guided by my feelings. In fact it wasn't until 1996 when Sapardi Djoko Damono wrote the introduction for *Di Luar Kata* (Beyond Words) I came to see that my poetry is, indeed, quite visual, with heavy doses of nature's description. This made me realize that in writing poetry, I was also painting. You can see this in some of earliest poems; in "Pangrango" and "Cipasung," for instance. But again, this was not something intentional, a strategy on my part per se. It was because those two sides of me—the writer and the painter—were developing at the same time.

ZH: You just said that writing poetry is painting with words but when an idea springs to your mind, what happens? Do you think, perhaps, that this idea would be best expressed in poetry or that idea would be better expressed on canvas?

AZN: For me, things that are lyrical or contemplative, including my thoughts about nature, are best expressed in poetry. When I want to shout or scream, that's when I paint. Paintings are more verbal, more in-your-face.

ZH: What with both your father and grandfather being highly-respected religious figures, you grew up in a religious environment. Yet the world of poetry is one of rebellion against restrictive norms. Thus, I must ask, did your environment provide support for or restrict the creative process for you as a poet?

AZN: I need to point out that there is, in fact, a close link between literacy, literature, and the pesantren. Keep in mind that in years past it was religious scholars who were writing books, particularly interpretations of or abridged versions of larger volumes. Many religious scholars also wrote nadhom, that form of poetry used to introduce children the names of the prophets.

My father was a very democratic person who didn't restrict me or demand that I had to be this way or that. He may not have given me overt support but he did nothing to dampen my creativity and in this passive way of his, by not forbidding me to do something, he must have agreed with my choices. In short, while my environment did not provide structural or formal support for my development as a writer and painter, it did not restrict me either.

ZH: The kind of literary work produced in pesantren is generally "classic" in nature, wouldn't you say? Look at the works of the Arab poet, Abu Nuwas, for instance, which are used to explain religious beliefs. Pesantren are known to accommodate Arabic literary work. Was this the case at your pesantren? Did Arabic language or literature influence your poetry?

AZN: Of course I studied Arabic at the pesantren where literary texts are used in the instruction of Arabic grammar. But much of the work of major poets like Abu Nuwas was translated into Sundanese as nadhoman—poems that are sung around the time of the fifth daily prayer. So it was,

I came to know his work in Sundanese and not in the original Arabic.

ZH: What about the syair? Have traditional Indonesian poetic forms influenced your work?

AZN: They have but it was quite a while before I came to see that my quatrains resemble traditional four-line syair.

ZH: Your 1989 poem, "Cipasung," shows a strong Sufic or romantic influence. You see in that poem respect towards nature as the teacher of humankind. Nature is the place for devotion and prayer. Nature is complete unto itself. This sentiment is also apparent in your 1980 poem, "Pangrango," which shows the wonder of youth towards nature and beauty. At the same time, however, in the earlier poem there is no in-depth analysis of nature as can be seen the later poem. How do you explain this development?

AZN: After graduating from high school and moving to Bandung to enroll in university I found a mentor, the author Saini KM. *Pikiran Rakyat*, the Bandung-based newspaper, had a regular column titled "Pertemuan Kecil" (Little Meetings) whose editor was Saini KM. There, he published not only poetry by writers both young and old, but also critical analyses. I learned a great deal from Saini through that column. I also learned from Goenawan Mohamad through his poems that were published in *Horison* and from Ramadhan KH through his long poem, "Priangan si Jelita" (Enchanting Priangan). In Bandung at that time there was a strong Islamic mystical movement and numerous books on Islam and mysticism were being published by Pustaka Salman—which is how I came to know the work of many Sufi poets. All this was part of my educational process.

From my earliest days as a writer I wrote about nature—how one had to explore the values that are found in nature, how nature is a multiplicity of verses whose interpretation must be separate from one's interpretation of verses in the Quran. I began to write Sufic poetry near the end of my years at the university and I wrote "Cipasung" after I had graduated but was still living in Bandung.

From where I was living in Bandung I could see, in the distance, Cipasung, which, at that time, was little more than a village surrounded by mountains and rice fields. I would gaze at Mount Galunggung and the rice fields below. Those sights and my own memories of Cipasung stirred me to write that poem.

ZH: You mentioned having learned from Saini KM through his column in *Pikiran Rakyat*. Could you expand on that? What kind of method of instruction did he employ?

AZN: I had begun to read *Pikiran Rakyat* when I was still in high school in Cipasung. In fact, Saini KM published a number of my early poems in his column and discussed them therein. One thing interesting about Saini is that in his essays he not only taught literary theory; he also put stress on a poet's mental needs. This, I think, is something very important.

Studying poetry with Saini was like studying ethics (*akhlak*) or mysticism (*tasawuf*). For instance, a poet is not created but is born or gives birth to himself as a poet. Sure, there are certain stratagem that can be used to "create" a poet but, in time, these will likely fail and he will return to his former self.

Poetry is not a means for seeking fame or wealth. Poetry is a quiet space where you come to know yourself, where you can reflect on your own ruminations. That is one lesson I totally absorbed, much more so than any literary theory.

Saini also stressed that one didn't have to be a poet to love poetry; it was enough to appreciate poetry. Beware of becoming a fast-sprouting grass or a weed, as it were, whose too-rapid growth can deprive itself of the very nutrients needed for it to thrive. One can't force oneself to become a poet.

ZH: Did Saini also provide insight on how to write a good poem?

AZN: He touched on that—on the need for a poet not to be overly productive. "Productivity" can be a good thing, he contended, but there are also risks involved: of forcing oneself to be productive, the use of mannerisms, repetition, and so on.

ZH: Going back to the poem, "Cipasung," you mentioned that at the time you wrote the poem there was an active Sufi movement in Bandung. Were you part of that movement or just using a Sufic style in your writing?

AZN: The latter—but not so much in terms of form. It was because I was reading Sufi poetry at that time, the works of Rumi and Hafiz. Theirs is a much more narrative or verbal approach. I wasn't very much influenced by that; I was more attracted to their content, how to reflect on the world, how nature is created, not on poetic forms. Whatever the case, one has to remember that these Sufi poets were known as Sufi religious leaders before becoming known as poets. Their poems were tools for the conveyance of Sufic teachings. It wasn't their view that poetry must contain lessons or must say something. Poems should, rather, incite reflection. My approach is closer to that.

ZH: I'd like now to ask you about the time when when you were an art student in Italy. How did that come about?

AZN: I had a painting exhibit at C-Line Gallery in Jakarta and one of the guests at the opening was the ambassador of Italy to Indonesia. He bought one of my paintings and then recommended me for a scholarship to study in Italy.

My time as a student from 1991 to 1993 at the University of Stranieri in Perugia was a very exciting time for me, especially in terms of my writing which became much more visual as a result of that experience. The area in which I lived in Umbria somewhat resembled the Priangan region. Previously, I had thought about nature, of course, but there, in Umbria, nature seemed to come alive for me. As a result, my poems became increasingly visual.

ZH: The poem "Above Umbria," is one of my favourite poems from your "Italian period." That poem and others from the period reveal an explosion of new imagery. How did this come about? Were you reading more?

AZN: In Italy I was able to find books by poets whose names I only knew before—books in English, Spanish, and Italian. Even though my foreign language skills were no more than rudimentary at the time, I bought the books anyway—a kind of experiment for myself, something akin to the tradition at the pesantren where books are held in high esteem. Books are meant not just to be read but to be treated with respect. Books provide positive energy to the person who treats them with respect.

I bought lots of books of poetry. I felt them with my hands; I smelled their scent, their yellow paper. At first,

I could barely understand them and could only imagine what they might saying but maybe it was that I absorbed their influence in a spiritual way. Later, after I had gained some fluency in Italian I did begin to translate the work of Octavio Paz. I also read Pablo Neruda and Dylan Thomas in the original. I smelled their books as I had the books at the pesantren when I was a boy.

What's clear is that at that time I was living in a breath-taking setting which excited my own imagination. What I saw and I felt combined to become the poems that I produced during that time. In a sense, my poems were a continuum of my visual and spiritual experiences. With my eyes, I'd see a train track, old buildings, churches and but I was at the same time feeling other things in my soul. A kind of fusion took place and, with that, a shift from the previous period exemplified by the poem "Cipasung."

ZH: You mentioned Octavio Paz. For me, the juxtaposition of images in your poems from the Umbria period seems to resemble the juxtaposition of imagery in Paz's poems. Had you begun to study Octavio Paz or was this because of something else?

AZN: In 1990, the year before I went to Italy to study, Paz won the Nobel Prize in Literature, after which a number of his poems appeared in Indonesian translation in *Horison*. They impressed me greatly and made me want to study and to translate his work.

ZH: Speaking of "translation," how did you determine your choice of poems for this collection? What was behind your selection of poems for this particular volume?

AZN: As this is meant to be a historical anthology, I chose poems from all my published titles, from the earliest to the latest.

I first put them together in chronological order and then arranged them by theme. In the end, I think I came up with a fairly representative selection.

ZH: Did the fact that the audience for this collection is the English-language reader influence your choice? I mean, did you choose poems in which Indonesia or your birthplace was highlighted, for instance?

AZN: No, as I said, I used a chronological approach but then, in the end, chose only poems I thought were most successful.

ZH: We spoke earlier of poets who influenced your creative development as a poet. Do you think you have had an influence on younger poets of Indonesia?

AZN: Whether that is the case would be for someone else to judge. I established a literary community and I teach poetry-writing but I don't use my own poems as a standard for my students to follow. I let them search for and develop forms of their own.

ZH: For me, the late 1990s, the period after you wrote the poems that would appear in *Di Atas Umbria* (Above Umbria) was an important one for Indonesian literature. Towards the end of the Soeharto regime in 1998, the social-political atmosphere had become increasingly heated and Indonesian authors were responding accordingly, both then as well as after Soeharto's fall. In prose, for instance, Seno Gumira Ajidarma's fictional work moved between surrealism and social protest. Similarly, your 2001 collection, *Dongeng dari Negeri Sembako* (Tales from the Country of Nine Basic Food Supplies) is marked by a tone of social protest. What do you say to this?

AZN: That particular collection can be seen as a new development
        in my poetry but also an aberration of sorts. Here's the
        context.... After the fall of Soeharto's, rioting broke out
        in Tasikmalaya and stores were burnt. The effects of the
        rioting were very bad, so I and other like-minded writers
        and artists formed a community to respond. One thing
        we did was to start a kasidah group—a kind of poetry
        recitation group—called "Nurul Sembako" (The Light
        of Nine Basic Food Supplies) which went on to perform
        throughout the region.

        I created the lyrics for the kasidah that were performed.
        Initially, the lyrics were very short, ones that could be sung
        the way a kasidah is usually sung. In doing this, I was
        responding to the social-political atmosphere in a tongue-
        in-cheek sort of way, the way it's done in Sundanese
        tales (*dongeng*) which are peppered with disjointed but
        humorous remarks.

        The poems that came to be published in that collection
        first appeared as texts on banners we put up in Tasikmalaya.
        I wasn't calling them poems at that time. They were song
        texts—ones that were very much linked to that particular
        time and place—that were to be sung in a playful manner
        to the accompaniment of a tambourine. Perhaps there
        are some among them that people might now consider to
        have a universal understanding but, once again, they were
        all very much linked to that particular time and place.

ZH: As a result of your activities, did you come under any
        pressure from other parties, from pro-Soeharto supporters,
        for instance?

AZN: After the fall of Soeharto and the beginning of the
        Reformasi period, there appeared in Tasikmalaya—as

elsewhere in the country—numerous outsiders or agitators as it were. There were religious groups who, in the name of religion, felt free to do whatever they wished. There were groups of turban-topped demonstrators, the likes of which we had never seen before, protesting against anything and everything. Towards this phenomenon, I fought back through art—through the kasidah and banners I mentioned previously.

In Tasikmalaya, there were certain parties who wanted to enact syariah law. We fought back against this movement with humor. For instance, one of my banners read, "With an Islamic religious vision, let us popularize polygamy" (Dengan visi religius-Islami, kita masyarakatkan poligami). That kind of thing really got things going in Tasikmalaya, and not just among the general public. Women's organizations came out in force. Meanwhile, the mass media reported on it as if there was a pro-polygamy campaign in Tasikmalaya whereas, in fact, we were criticizing those politicians who were calling for syariah law—because, in fact, the only the part of syariah law they wanted was the part where polygamy is permitted.

ZH: So, poetry versus politics.... What's your opinion?

AZN: In my mind, there is no connection between the two; they are diametrically opposed. Politicians and poets are of two completely different minds. Poetry can respond to social-political situations but should not become a part of it, much less be used by politicians. The poems in *Dongeng dari Negeri Sembako* are in fact comments on the misguided actions of parliamentarians, the governor, and other political leaders.

ZH: Sapardi Djoko Damono once said, "If you are angry, don't write poetry." What I see this meaning is that one must first ingest what is causing us anger and only then write about it.

AZN: I see two ways of dealing with that particular emotion: one is through the use of humor as I did in *Dongeng dari Negeri Sembako*; the other is to write poetry that is more narrative in nature, in which one can slip in social commentary, as I did in another collection, *Bagian dari Kegembiraan* (A Part of Joy). But I agree, poetry is not a vehicle for anger. In poetry, we must to be able to make fun of ourselves.

ZH: And today, are you still using the poetic model found in *Dongeng dari Negeri Sembako*?

AZN: To a certain extent, I am. Following the mass protest by Islamist groups against the Jakarta governor in 2016 when he was accused of blasphemy, I wrote about the protests, but in haiku format. Those poems appeared in my 2019 collection, *Tonggeret*.

ZH: Haiku? For a modern poet like you, what is it that attracted you to haiku?

AZN: Of late, I've gone back to back to traditional forms of poetry: the syair, quatrain, sonnet, and haiku as examples. This has been part of the meditative process for me. Having explored freedom of form, I now feel the need to go back to writing poems with a regular, even rigid, structure. For the past five years now I have been working on these forms.

        Most haiku contain the writer's view about nature, which relates closely with what I've been doing all this time. There's a connection. In this day and age, which for me is very "technical-oriented," it's very difficult to make use of metaphors. Sometimes I just play around—that's my free haiku. All this is a part of experimentation—with short words and no metaphoric embellishment, which is a true challenge to do.

ZH: These days, what is it as a poet that you find most unnerving?

AZN: What unnerves me now is the same as what unnerved me in the past and poetry, for me, is a way out from those feelings, a way to transform such feelings into poetic work.

ZH: On a final note, I'd like to ask what you might have to say about the state of the world of poetry in Indonesia today.

AZN: Indonesian literature has grown in leaps and bounds as a result of technological developments. But the digital world for me is only a form of media, an instrument. Real literature, beautiful literature, requires serious work. Likely, the process is the same as in previous generations. The only thing is that while before, literature was written on stone, metal, or palm leaf, and later poetry, in this digital era, development has been even more rapid. Even so, good literature still needs serious work, not just quick production. "Digital" is merely a tool.

Biographical Information

Acep Zamzam Noor (born 1960) is a poet and painter who was born in Tasikmalaya, West Java. Growing up in a traditional religious environment, he was educated first at a *pesantren* not far from his home town but during his high school years attended the As-Syafi'iyah *pesantren* in Jakarta. Thereafter, he enrolled as a student in the Faculty of Visual Arts and Design at the Bandung Institute of Technology (Institut Teknologi Bandung/ITB), one of Indonesia's top three arts institutes. Several years after his graduation from ITB in 1987, he then studied at Universita Italiana per Stranieri in Perugia (1991-1993) on a scholarship from the Italian government.

Acep writes both in Indonesian, the national language, and Sundanese, his mother tongue. He has published eight collections in the former language and three in the latter. His first prize for his poetry came in 2000 from the National Language Center of the Department of Education for a collection titled *Di Luar Kata* (Beyond Words) and in 2005 he was named recipient of the SEA-Write Award for Indonesia by the royal government of Thailand. In 2006 the government of West Java bestowed on him its highest award in the field of culture and in 2007 the Minister of Culture and Tourism awarded him a gold medal for his essays on culture that were published in the mass media. Also in 2007, his Indonesian-language collection titled *Menjadi Penyair Lagi* (A Poet Once More) garnered for him the Khatulistiwa Literary Award for poetry, Indonesia's most esteemed literary award. He won this same award again for his 2013 collection titled *Bagian dari Kegembiraan* (A Part of Joy) which also won for him first prize for best poetry collection on National Poetry Day that year. On National Poetry Day in 2017, he won first prize again, this time for his collection title *Berguru Kepada Rindu* (Lessons from Longing). His 2011 Sundanese-language collection titled *Paguneman* (Conversations) was the recipient of the Rancagé Literary Award, a literary award specifically given to works in several of the regional languages of Indonesia.

Acep has previously had one collection of poems appear in English and German, that being *Death Approaching and Other Poems* (The Lontar Foundation, 2015) and another, in French, titled *Ailleurs Des Mots* (Sorbonne Nouvelle, 2016). Individual titles have been translated into a wide range of other languages.

JOHN H MCGLYNN is a co-founder of the Lontar Foundation, a non-profit organization established for the purpose of introducing Indonesia to the world through literary translations. Through Lontar, McGlynn has ushered into print close to 250 books on Indonesian literature and culture with translations of literary work by more than 650 Indonesian authors. Because of Lontar's work, Indonesian literature can be taught anywhere in the world through the medium of English. As the translator of several dozen publications himself, both under his own name as well as his pen name, Willem Samuels, he has garnered much international praise for his work. His long list of publications include titles by some of Indonesia's most well known authors.